I'm Your Buddy

A True Story

Written by Carol Ann Rowell

Illustrated by Pamela Becker

To all winged ones, both in body and spirit. Birds have been depicted throughout history for their mystical and magical influences on humankind. These beings express grace, dignity and knowingness of purpose. All qualities to aspire to. —CAR

As the illustrator, being introduced to the feathered family of Carol and Gary Rowell has changed my life. Once you experience the lucid presence of a being that weighs less than one pound talking away directly to you, you understand a bit more clearly the connection of all things. —PB

Copyright © 2017 Carol Ann Rowell
Sedona, AZ

Cover and book illustration: Pamela Becker: www.bigvisionarts.com
Cover and book design: Naomi C. Rose: www.ncrdesigns.com

Text set in Gill Sans Infant Std

ISBN: 97809987142-1-9

Wings Up Publishing, LLC
Sedona, AZ
carolann@wingsuppublishing.com
www.wingsuppublishing.com

Introduction

I met Buddy at a pet store. As soon as I walked through the door, he greeted me in a voice that sounded like a cartoon bird.

"Wings up Buddy!" he shouted.

I turned my head his way.

"Come here," he said.

And so I did.

Buddy didn't look like other Goffin Cockatoos. He had pulled out most of his feathers. He looked almost bald all over, except for the feathers on his head. I guess, he didn't like his tail feathers either because he'd pulled them out as well.

But the way Buddy held his head up high, I could tell he only saw himself as a beautiful feathered bird.

I had to bring Buddy home with me. His loving, playful spirit had to be shared.

—CAR

So my story begins...

It's love at first sight!

I'm on my stand, dancing and singing "WINGS UP" at the pet store, like I always do. Suddenly I freeze. I can't take my eyes off a woman who has a big smile on her face.

"WINGS UP!" I shout in my loudest voice. Then I shout, "Buddy," so she knows my name. That gets her attention. I can tell she's really nice by the sweet look in her eyes. Maybe she'll take me home with her. "Come here," I say.

She comes right over, picks me up, and laughs. "Hello Honey," I put my head down so she can pet me.

"Oh Buddy Boy," she says, stroking my head with gentle fingers. "You are coming home with me and you can call me Mom."

Then I hear her calling home and saying, "Tell all the birds to look their best. I am coming home with a surprise."

Yippee!!!

Before I start my new life, I have to say goodbye to my friends.

My next-door neighbor, Barney, is my best friend. He wasn't a very happy bird when he arrived in the pet store. So I danced on his cage a lot and kept telling him, "WINGS UP!" That cheered him up a lot.

Now I say goodbye to Sunshine a yellow cockatiel who loves to lift her wings whenever I say, "WINGS UP!"

Next, I say goodbye to Joseph who is my newest friend in the pet store. I can tell they're all sad to see me go. I feel a little sad, too. I will miss my friends. I hope I'll have friends at my new house.

Mom puts me in a travel cage and then in the car, and off we go. I say, "Yeah Man." I learned that from Barney. Mom laughs.

Well, here we are at my new home. Mom takes me into the Bird Room. WOW what a surprise! Two brother birds and a sister bird live here. I hope they all like me.

Mom takes me around to each one.

First I meet Chico, an African Grey. Mom says he is forty years old and that is why he acts like the boss. I say, "WINGS UP."

But Chico just stares at me, shakes his head, and says nothing back. *Uh oh.* This isn't a good start to making new friends.

Next I meet Hunter, a Cockatiel. He's too busy sleeping to even look up. Scarlet, another African Grey, says, "So happy to see you."

Whew! At least someone likes me. "Hi Babe," I say, to let her know I want to be friends.

Mom puts me in my new cage.

WOW! It's got hanging bells, ribbons, and other fun toys. The dishes are full of my favorite seeds too. I have a lot of new things to check out. First I will have a bite to eat, but the bell is too tempting. I ring it again and again.

Hunter and Scarlett look up from their dishes and say, "WOW."

Chico doesn't say anything.

After a while, Mom takes us out of our cages and puts us on our stands. She switches on the TV to a music show. Chico and Scarlett sing and try to dance.

Hah! They don't have moves like mine. I dance tapping both feet, run around the stand, and sing my heart out.

I guess I get rather LOUD because Scarlett and Hunter turn their heads towards me with their beaks open.

Chico gives me his bossy stare.

Could it be they don't like my voice? No, it can't be that!

Mom says it's time to eat. She gives us pasta, corn, and carrots for dinner. *Yum.* I gobble it all up.

Chico says, "Thank You" to Mom.

How nice. I want to learn to say that too.

Dinner is done, the TV is off and Mom says it is bedtime. Mom puts us in our cages. She says to me, "Oh Buddy, I knew you were special, so happy you are one of my Peeps." Then she covers us up.

It's kind of dark in my cage with the cover on and that makes me sleepy. "Goodnight," says Mom. "I love you." I hear her throwing kisses. The other birds say "good night" and throw her kisses back. I do too.

As soon as Mom leaves the room, Chico and Scarlet pipe up. "Good night, good night," they say over and over.

Mom shouts from the hallway. "Okay birds go to bed." And that quiets everyone down.

I wake up early in the morning and scream, "WAKE UP!!!!!!!!!!!"

Mom races in, lifts my cover, and opens my cage. I jump to the top where I dip and dance. Mom laughs. "Well, GOOD MORNING BUDDY!" she says.

I jump on top of my cage and start dancing. The other birds stay silent even after they are uncovered. Guess they don't like a good morning wake up call.

Finally, Scarlett says, "Good morning," in a soft voice. But Chico's feathers are all puffed up. He must be REAL mad. I wonder if he'll ever be my friend.

"We'll eat breakfast outside," says Mom. Outside? What's that going to be like?

She takes us out to the patio and puts us on our stands and *Wow!!!* Music blares from outdoor speakers.

I love all kinds of music and I can dance to any beat. I have the moves. I can dip, jump, and tap both feet. I can go in circles too. I'm the only bird who can do all that. Maybe I can teach the other birds a move or two.

I find fruit and cereal in my dish. Well, I only like apples. So I throw out the grape and orange pieces.

Mom shakes her head. "Buddy, maybe tomorrow you will try some."

Chico says, "1-2-3-4-5-6." *Wow.* He's really smart. If we were friends, he could teach me to count, and I could teach him to say "WINGS UP."

Flapping my wings to get his attention I say, "WINGS UP!"

But he gives me his bossy stare and then turns his head away. I guess he is not ready to be friends yet.

After a few hours, we head back inside where Mom picks up a drum and starts beating it with a stick.

I'm not sure I like drumming, but soon I feel the beat and start to dance. Chico and Scarlett dance too and let out some loud sounds. They must have learned some of those dance moves from me already. But Chico would never admit it.

Mom keeps drumming and we all keep dancing. Except Hunter. I don't think he knows how to dance, because he just watches us. Then he lifts his wings and says, "Pretty Pretty Birdie." He's been doing that a lot. It's got to be his special talent. Every bird has one. That's what makes us so much fun.

Now what? Mom's taking us into the bathroom. When I see myself in the mirror, I scream. I have never seen myself before. I thought I had lots of feathers like the other birds.

Scarlet and Hunter say, "Pretty Bird," and I think they are talking to me. I now know I look different, but that's what makes me special. I say, "Pretty Bird," back.

Mom turns on the shower. I am NOT going to like this! Mom showers the others birds first and they like it.

Oh no! It's my turn. The water feels warm and soft. *Hey!* I like this after all.

I lift up my wings so Mom can shower me better. "Wings Up," I say.

After the shower, we go back to our stands in the living room. When Mom gives us dinner, I say, "Thank You."

I think Chico really likes that. Because later when Mom picks me up and hugs me, Chico says a big, "AH," like he approves that I'm getting some loving from Mom. After that he stops giving me bossy stares.

Even better, when Mom takes us into the bedroom, Chico says, "GOODNIGHT BUDDY."

Yay. We're finally friends! I say "Good Night" back and throw him a kiss.

Well this day is over and it is time for bed.

Mom covers us up and blows us kisses. "Good Night, see you in the morning," the other birds say to Mom and I throw her a kiss and say, "Good Night."

Chico starts saying, "I am praying for a miracle." I think my miracle is living here, and having Chico and the gang LOVE me like I love them.

Well, boys and girls (and any birds that might be reading this book), I hope you enjoyed my story and that you continue to lift your wings and join me and say, "WINGS UP!" which means *Be the Best You Can Be.*

Be happy.

Hug yourself.

Say thank you often.

And remember you are special just the way you are.

I'M YOUR BUDDY!

My next book will be Me and the birds going on a road trip.

See you then!

True and Funny Bird Talk

I'm so happy to see you.

How are you doing?

Happy birthday to me.

I love you Babe.

Do you want to go outside?

I love you Peep.

I'm the best bird in the whole world.

Pardon me.

Think about it.

Mommy, what are you doing?

Do you want a treat?

Do you need some help?

Tell me more.

I'm freezing.

I got to go to bed, see you in the morning.

About the Author

For the past 28 years, with the support of Gary, her husband, Carol Ann Rowell has rescued many neglected and abused birds and made them a part of their family. The birds are varied in appearance and personality, but accept each other and have become a flock. They have opened Carol and Gary's hearts and quieted their minds, allowing their childlike joy to manifest. Their message is "Wings Up No Matter What" as they experience life with acceptance and love.

About the Illustrator

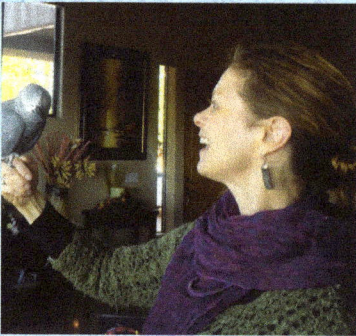

Illustrator, fine artist and designer, Pamela Becker is a long time Sedona, Arizona resident and owner of Big Vision Art + Design. She's illustrated over 30 children's books for small and large publications alike. A Rhode Island School of Design alumna, her fine art has been collected world wide. Extensive global travel and the experience of a variety of cultures and societies has given her work the patina of diversity, the essence of wonder, and a broader scope of vision.

About The Oasis Sanctuary

For nearly two decades, The Oasis Sanctuary, a 501(c)(3) nonprofit avian welfare organization has been a safe haven for unwanted, aged, neglected, injured and special needs parrots. For countless birds, The Oasis is their last option and offers a new beginning. As a true Sanctuary, The Oasis does not breed, adopt out, sell or trade birds. Once a bird enters the doors of The Oasis, they are guaranteed a lifetime of care and compassion. We assess each individual bird to provide optimum care including a healthy diet, medical care, opportunities for flight and flock socialization in natural aviary environments. Our first priority is, and will remain, the long-term care, well-being and safety of the birds entrusted to our care. www.the-oasis.org. *10% of Net Proceeds from each book will be donated to The Oasis Bird Sanctuary.*

www.ingramcontent.com/pod-product-compliance
Lightning Source LLC
Chambersburg PA
CBHW040251100426
42811CB00011B/1225